Joseph Augustus Seiss

The Assassinated President

Or the Day of National Mourning for Abraham Lincoln

Joseph Augustus Seiss

The Assassinated President
Or the Day of National Mourning for Abraham Lincoln

ISBN/EAN: 9783337041984

Printed in Europe, USA, Canada, Australia, Japan

Cover: Foto ©ninafisch / pixelio.de

More available books at **www.hansebooks.com**

The Assassinated President,

OR THE

DAY OF NATIONAL MOURNING

FOR

ABRAHAM LINCOLN,

AT

ST. JOHN'S (LUTHERAN) CHURCH, PHILADELPHIA,

JUNE 1st, 1865.

THE PASTOR,

JOSEPH A. SEISS, D. D.,

OFFICIATING.

FOR SALE AT

No. 42 NORTH NINTH STREET,

PHILADELPHIA.

1865.

"The tyrannous and bloody act is done;
The most arch deed of piteous massacre,
That ever yet this land was guilty of."

I. THE DEVOTIONAL EXERCISES.

INTROIT.—" Let the words of my mouth, and the meditation of my heart, be acceptable in thy sight, O Lord, my Strength and my Redeemer."

Reading of the Ten Commandments, Ex. 20 : 1—17.

THE CONFESSION OF SINS.

ALMIGHTY and most holy Lord and God, who dost command us to humble ourselves under thy mighty hand, that thou mayest exalt us in due time ; in humility of spirit we confess before thee, in this our bereavement and affliction, how deeply, as a nation, we have deserved thy wrath. We acknowledge thy righteousness in the sorrowful visitation which has come upon us, and bow to thy holy will in submission and self-abasement. Manifold are our transgressions, and the more sinful because of the many and great mercies which thou hast bestowed upon us. We have sinned, in pride and living to ourselves, in covetousness and worldliness of mind, in self-sufficiency and too much trusting in man instead of thee.

Profaneness of speech, violation and disregard of thy holy day, neglect of thy worship, unbelief and contempt of thy word, unfaithfulness to public trusts, dishonesties in worldly business, and above all, receiving in vain thy wonderful grace in the Gospel of our Lord Jesus Christ, all cry out for thy indignation and wrath. It is because thy compassions have not failed, that we have not been consumed. We adore the riches of thy forbearance and long-suffering; and beseech thee, O Lord, to turn the hearts of this people to repentance and supplication, that still thou mayest have compassion upon us; not weighing our merits, but pardoning our offences. For thy Son, our Lord Jesus Christ's sake, forgive us all that is past, and grant that ever hereafter we may all serve and please thee in newness of life, to the honor and glory of thy name, through him who liveth and reigneth with thee and the Holy Ghost, ever one God, world without end. Amen.

HYMN.

"Great Maker of unnumbered worlds,
And whom unnumbered worlds adore,
Whose goodness all thy creatures share,
While nature trembles at thy power," &c.

SCRIPTURE LESSONS.—Isaiah 59, and Luke 6 : 20—38.

THE GENERAL PRAYER.

Almighty and most merciful God, we lift our hearts to thee, the hearer of prayer, from whom alone cometh our help. We adore thee as the great Parent of the Universe, from whom all things proceed, and on whom all creatures depend. Thou art worthy of all honor, gratitude, affection, and obedience. Thou art the blessed and only Potentate, the King of kings, and Lord of lords. Thou alone hast immortality. With thee are the issues of life and of death. Thou doest after the counsels of thine own will among the angels in heaven and in the affairs of men. We, thine unworthy servants, desire to recognize thy hand in all things, and to be duly grateful to thee for thy many and great mercies. We bless thee for our creation, preservation; and all the comforts and privileges of this life. As citizens of a country which thou hast highly favored, as well as sorely chastised, we adore thee for what thou hast done for us, and humbly submit ourselves to thy holy governance. We adore thee for all the way which thou hast led us, in darkness and in light, in defeats and in victories, in days of discouragements and days of rejoicing, and for all the lessons which thou art in all addressing to us. We bless thee for the steadfast devotion and obedience of the people to the Government, under their many burdens during these years of trial. We thank thee that when dangerous conspiracies arose, thou didst bring them to nought. We thank thee that no invasions of loyal territory have been permitted to prosper; and that, in so large a part of the land, there have been preserved to us tranquillity and prosperity, abundance of the fruits of the ground, and the undisturbed enjoyment of the means of grace. We thank thee for the devotion and bravery and patience and faithfulness of the national forces, on land and water, through whose skill and courage thou hast wrought such great things for us; beseeching thee to return them to their homes in safety, to give them all happiness in their families, to fill their hearts with love to thee, and to bring them finally to the blessedness of thy kingdom. And we pray thee so to impress the hearts of all the nation with a just sense of thy providence, goodness, and mercy in the years just passed, and in our present deliverance and prospects, that all may most thankfully acknowledge their debt of love and praise, and serve thee henceforth in humble obedience to thy word.

And as thou hast seen fit, O thou mighty Ruler of the world, in thine all-wise administrations, to permit us to be deprived of the presence and further counsels of our late Chief Magistrate, and hast so deeply grieved the hearts of the people, turning our songs into mourning and our joy into sorrow; we beseech thee to have mercy upon us in this our calamity, and to overrule it to the furtherance of our humility and peace, and to thine everlasting glory. Give unto us the gracious aid of thy Holy Spirit, that we may rightly learn thy will, and profit by all thy dealings with us. Enable us to have a right estimate of the good example and timely services vouchsafed to us in the life of him whom thou hast taken, and to be governed aright in all our feelings and meditations concerning the same. We thank thee for the great grace and faithfulness thou gavest him in his high office, and for the success with which thou hast favored his administrations to the preservation of our national unity and the enlargement of human freedom, and beseech thee to help us to appreciate the high trusts which thou hast by him regiven to our keeping. Have compassion upon his sorrowing family and relatives, whom thou hast called to endure this sore bereavement. Cause their hearts to be lifted toward thy grace for support and consolation. Mingle the ministrations of thy love with the bitterness of their cup. Grant them, in this cloud of darkness, to see and rejoice in the light of life; and lead them by thy heavenly grace to life everlasting.

And for him who, by this mysterious providence, is now called to assume the highest office in the nation, we entreat thy protection, support, and guidance. Teach him where to look for all he needs under the heavy duties which have come upon him, and give him grace so to administer the Government after the good example which has been set before him, that by wisdom and moderation, by firmness and clemency, in the due vindication of justice and remembrance of mercy, the laws may be truly honored, the wounds of the nation healed, and peace and unity restored to the land for all generations.

We implore thy blessing upon our entire country, and upon all its inhabitants. Have compassion, O Lord, upon those regions which war has desolated, and in which the weapons of rebellion were lifted. Restore to them thy gracious favor. May the waste places be made to bloom again. Give to the erring and the vanquished the spirit of loyal submission to the rightful authority of the nation. Heal the wounds that have been made in their homes and neighborhoods, in their peace and prosperity. Take away from them and from us all bitterness, wrath, and anger, and make us all kind one toward another. Make us again one people, not only by union under the same laws, but in affectionate participation in the same national privileges; serving together in the one faith of thy holy word, working together for the advancement of the one glorious kingdom of righteousness and peace, and inheritors together of eternal life, through the one sacrifice and mediation of our Lord and Saviour Jesus Christ.

Let it please thee, also, to help and bless all sorts and conditions of men, making thy ways known unto them, and saving them from their sins. Endow all rulers and magistrates with thy grace, and fill them with the spirit of wisdom and justice. Show thy goodness to the sorrowing and afflicted, and give deliverance to the enslaved and oppressed. Remember thy Church in tender mercy, and refresh and prosper it with the continual dew of thy heavenly blessing. Send down upon all ministers of the Gospel, and upon all thy people, the needful Spirit of thy grace. Cause the number of thy saints to be multiplied in all the earth; and let thy blessed kingdom speedily come, and thy holy will be done on earth as it is in heaven.

Hear us, most gracious Lord and God, and despise not these our unworthy services, neither deny us our requests, which we present before thy Divine Majesty in the name of Jesus Christ, our Mediator and Redeemer, to whom, with thee, and the Holy Ghost, be all honor and glory, world without end.

AMEN.

SECOND HYMN.

"God moves in a mysterious way,
His wonders to perform ;
He plants his footsteps in the sea,
And rides upon the storm," &c.

II. THE DISCOURSE.

TEXT.—"And Moses was an hundred and twenty years old when he died: his eye was not dim, nor his natural force abated. And the children of Israel wept for Moses in the plains of Moab thirty days." *Deut.* 33 : 7, 8.

MANY-SIDED, and full of light, are even the simplest records of the word of God. This little historic fragment is rich in fruitful themes for solemn meditation. Even in the line of thinking to which the appointment of this day specially calls us, there are sundry very noteworthy suggestions.

We here find that the most eminent servants of God, as well as other people, are subject to the dominion of death.

We here find that men high in office and favor, are sometimes suddenly taken away in the fulness of their strength, in the midst of their labors and usefulness, just when their presence seems most indispensable, and on the very eve of the consummation of their most earnest endeavors.

We here find that from remote antiquity, from

some motive of religion, or praiseworthy impulse of justice, gratitude, or admiration, it has been the custom of good people to take special notice of the deaths of distinguished public servants, to express by unwonted tokens the sense of loss sustained by their removal, and to give befitting indications of appreciation of their qualities and worth on the part of their survivors.

But I do not propose to dwell on these topics. I mention them, as I use the text itself, not for discussion, but chiefly as a preface and starting-point for other observations. The mention of Moses, the close of his career, and the mourning of the people for him, calls up the character and mission of Moses. These, connected with the purposes for which we are this day in the sanctuary, naturally suggest the comparison of this illustrious personage with him over the recent, sudden, and melancholy termination of whose life the nation mourns, and the civilized world is moved.

Who Moses was needs scarcely to be stated. His history is written in the best known and most sacred books of nearly all nations, and is familiar to the children of almost every home. His origin among a people who labored in the brickyards and served the Egyptians, his inheritance of hardships deserved neither by him nor his parents, and his providential preservation in early infancy, are things which we learned in the first lessons of our childhood. You remember how he was committed to his mother to be nursed and reared for Pharaoh's daughter, whose maids had found him in the river. You know from whose lips he was taught in the traditions and religion of his people, and whence he drank in those sentiments of justice, faith in God, sympathy with the oppressed, and love of freedom and equal rights, which manifested themselves so strikingly in his early manhood, and became the guiding-star of his life and greatness. You do not need to be told what office it was that he was called to fill, and how he was gradually schooled for it by his training in Egyptian learning, by his military experiences in an expedition against the depredatory tribes of Ethiopia, in his voluntary exile from the place of his birth, in his servitude and quiet meditations as keeper of Jethro's flocks, and in his sharp and prolonged contest with the Magicians of Pharaoh's court. Nor will it ever be forgotten how he humbled the pride of them that withstood him, and gathered to himself the confidence of the people, and submitted himself to the promptings of his conscience, and enraged Egypt's haughty aristocrats with his proposals and demands in behalf of the oppressed, and in the face of Egypt's armies led out the enslaved from the house of bondage, and saw the hosts of Israel's oppressors overwhelmed under

the waving of his staff, and silenced the murmurs
of the rebellious in his own camp, and rewrote and
reasserted the great laws of right, loyalty, and justice, and forced his way through lands which he had
been forbidden to pass, and was tried by the treach-
erous schemes of Balak and Baalam, and vanquished the tribes who took up arms against his people,
and conducted Israel through the wilderness to the
very borders of the land of rest, and then suddenly
ended his career, as he had been forewarned, amid
the tears and lamentations of those whom he had
delivered and led.

And how closely all this resembles the story of *his*
life, for whom this national mourning has been ap-
pointed, scarcely requires to be pointed out. If
Moses was of humble parentage, so was he. His
father was a poor Kentuckian, who could neither
read nor write; and his mother was a lowly woman,
whose highest literary attainment was ability to read
her Bible. If Moses derived from his mother those
sentiments and feelings which formed the basis of
his exalted character and success, the same may be
said of the late President. Though uneducated, his
mother was a talented woman, of sound practical
wisdom, earnest piety, and great devotion to her son;
and to her influence and teachings, many of the
traits which distinguished his life are traced by his
biographers. A child of poverty and hardships, he

was early expatriated from the place of his birth, transferred to the wilderness, subsisted on scanty fare, and made to serve strangers. Though not " learned in all the wisdom of the Egyptians," and obliged to borrow the books from which he obtained the first rudiments of his literary knowledge, he was thoroughly educated in the school of humble life, and familiarized with all its necessities and trials, which, in his case, as in that of Moses, was the most valuable part of his education. He, too, was a captain and soldier in a campaign against tribes of marauding savages. He, too, found it a great turning point in his life, when, in answer to the generous impulses of his heart, he volunteered to stand between an innocent sufferer and his accusers, and rescued him from a death which he had not merited. And if the controlling sympathies of Moses ran with the injured, the wronged, and the enslaved, such was exactly the temper of Abraham Lincoln, who, also, at an early period, gave decisive evidence of his utter contempt for the preferments and luxuries of enslaving power. He, too, was born to figure in a great crisis in the affairs of his country, and remarkably called to execute a mission as pregnant with results as it was feeble in friends, resources, and promises of success. Even the complaint which the Jewish leader uttered with reference to the apparent inadequacy of the instrument to the end to be accomplished, had its correspondence in him for whom we this day mourn. "Who am I," said he, "that I should go unto Pharoah, and that I should bring forth the children of Israel out of Egypt"—"O my Lord, I am not eloquent." (Ex. 3 : 11 ; 4 : 10.)

And that great debate, of which all the people of Illinois were the witnesses, and in which all sections of the country were unwontedly interested; in which he was resisted by perhaps the most formidable champion of the political arena then living; in which all the powers of extraordinary genius, adroitness, and forensic skill were brought to bear against him; and which first fully laid open the question of freedom and slavery which the God of battles has since decided in his favor;—what was it but a re-enactment upon another theatre, and in another form, of that contest between the shepherd of Midian and the Magicians of Egypt? Indeed, contemplated from almost any point, the considerate mind will be at no loss to trace resemblances between his character and career and that of the matchless man whom the Scriptures set before us as the great hero of Israel's deliverance.

Nor were the times and circumstances in which the two were called to operate, very dissimilar. By some strange forgetfulness of acknowledged rights and covenants, there had been a power put forth in Egypt, by which the multiplied posterity of Jacob were divested of their freedom, and subjected to rigorous taskmasters, "who made their lives bitter with hard bondage, in mortar and in brick, and in all manner of service in the field." (Ex. 1 : 8–14.) " And the children of Israel sighed by reason of the bondage, and they cried, and their cry came up unto God. And God heard their groaning. And God looked upon the children of Israel, and God had respect unto them." (Ex. 2 : 23–25.) In other words, the time had come, in the decrees of Heaven, when the heavy yoke was to be broken, the pride of the oppressor humbled, and these suffering tribes set free.

So, on this continent, a new power in the world had risen up, in the Constitution of which, owing to whatever causes, or modified by whatever apologies, contrary to the convictions and desires of its framers, elements of oppression and undoubted wrong had been embodied and legalized, by which millions of human beings, brought hither in their misfortunes, were doomed to abject and unqualified servitude;— a servitude which, however mild, gentle, and benficent in some cases and relations, or excusable on the part of those who had no share in producing it, did embrace, in its very nature, a violation of the common rights of man, and was everywhere attended more or less with hardships and horrors, for which the inexorable requirements of justice demanded that a day of retributive revolution should come. To such a pass had things been carried, that, in some sections of the land, there was not a day in which human souls were not bought and transported as common chattels, and families severed without compunctions, and nameless crimes perpetrated without the possibility of redress; whilst the whole population of all the States was put under requirements to aid in holding tight the bonds of the unoffending, and in remanding to their toils and miseries such as had sufficient human feeling left to seek for freedom by their flight. What the founders of our institutions regarded and lamented as a wrong to the bondman and an evil to the state, had come to be accepted and defended as the sublimest beneficence, the foundation of liberties, and the proper basis of republican government; nay, as the very ordination of Almighty Goodness, to touch or question which was considered treason to the country and sin against God. The enlargement and consolidation of enslaving power had come to be the engrossing object of national legislation, and the making firm of slave bonds the great test of patriotism. The press, the rostrum, and the pulpit, were being largely subsidized to the same interest; and the free speech of men who failed in the pronunciation of its Shiboleth, in nearly every section of the country, was put under ban, and held obnoxious to all the penalties of this world and of that which is to come. Long had the nation submitted and yielded to the ever-multiplying demands of the "peculiar institution," until the God of justice said, "*It is too much,*" and gave commission to his angels to strike it down, yea, and to sweep it from the earth.

While Egypt was busy riveting the fetters tighter and tighter upon Israel, little did she dream that, within her own borders, there was a young mind maturing, who, with no ally but God, and no supports but the righteousness of his cause, was presently to scatter all her infamous legislation to the winds. Little did she think, that, from among the poor and despised whom her tyranny was oppressing, there was one gradually being prepared, upon whose plain unvarnished words should follow consternating judgments, before which the pride of her dominion was to be laid level with the dust. And little did she imagine how, from the wilds of Midian, there was presently to come a sun-browned shepherd, by whose calm administrations all her great houses were to be filled with mourning, stript of their illgot treasures, and deprived forever of the unrequited services of those on the sins against whose manhood her haughty ones had fattened and exulted. But, when God wanted a Moses, there was a Moses ready, hidden away far back in the desert of Horeb, and who, in due time, received his commission from among the trees of the wilderness.

The same has been repeated, in our day, in our country. The picture rises to your view without my aid to call it up.

*   *   *   *   *   *   *   *

One of the most controlling features in the character of Moses, which shines out in his whole career, undimmed by a single stain of inconsistency, was his self-sacrificing devotion to his convictions of justice and right, based upon his religious faith. His inspired eulogist has said of him, and meant in this to sum up the great actuating principle of his life, that he " chose rather to suffer affliction with the people of God than to enjoy the pleasures of sin for a season, esteeming the reproach of Christ greater riches than the treasures in Egypt; for he had respect unto the recompense of the reward." (Heb. 10 : 24–28.)

The same is, in a large measure, true of our late Chief Magistrate. Though not, so far as I am informed, a professed Christian, at least not in all particulars, he was a man of decided religious turn of mind, who lived and acted in the light and influence of a practical faith. It was from his religious persuasions that all his ideas were shapen, and according to which he honestly sought to settle his judgment and direct his course, whether in matters of private life or of public policy. All his opinions thus came to partake of the nature of religious principles, which no personal hazards or counter motives could induce him for one moment to forsake, and for which he was willing to assume any amount of responsibility, and to submit to any degree of self-sacrifice. He died a martyr's death, but only because he was pervaded from the beginning with the elements of a martyr's spirit. He had learned, from the holiest authority, that God "hath made of one blood all nations of men," and that the immutable rule of right, as between man and man, is to do unto others as we would that they should do unto us. And his entire career, in all his public acts at least, was simply the earnest and honest application of these principles. Hence his uniform and generous sympathy with the oppressed and the suffering. Hence his early protest, upon the records of his State, in which he declared it to be his solemn belief, " that the institution of slavery is founded on both injustice and bad policy." Hence his advocacy, in Congress, of the right of petition for its removal, his votes to exclude it from the Territories where it had not yet been planted, his efforts to have it abolished in the District of Columbia, his indignation at the repeal of the Missouri Compromise, his ever-deepening abhorrence of the whole system, and his consent to undertake the leadership of an effort to withstand its insatiable encroachments, and to carry his principles into a national administration which had neither precedents nor records to guide it, and which the great mass of those in power stood pledged to resist.

Nor did he count anything too dear to be laid upon the altar of that cause, which he believed to be the cause of humanity and of God. Nobler words, and revealing the whole structure of his moral thinking, perhaps were never uttered by man, than those in which he said to the people of Illinois:

"The thirteen colonies, by their representatives in old Independence Hall, said to the world of men, 'We hold these truths to be self-evident, that all men are born equal; that they are endowed by their Creator with certain inalienable rights; that among these are life, liberty, and the pursuit of happiness.' This was their lofty and wise and noble understanding of the justice of the Creator to His creatures,—to the whole great family of man. In their belief, nothing stamped with the Divine image and likeness was sent into the world to be trodden on, and degraded and imbruted by its fellows. They grasped not only the race of men then living, but they reached forward and seized upon the furthest posterity. They created a beacon to guide their children, and their children's children, and the countless myriads who should inhabit the earth in other ages. Wise statesmen as they were, they knew the tendency of prosperity to breed tyrants; and so they established these great self-evident truths, that when, in the distant future, some man, some faction, some interest, should set up the doctrine that none but rich men, or none but white men, or none but Anglo-Saxon white men, were entitled to life, liberty, and the pursuit of happiness, their posterity might look up again to the Declaration of Independence, and take courage to renew the battle which their fathers began, so that truth and justice and mercy, and all the humane and Christian virtues, might not be extinguished from the land; so that no man would hereafter dare to limit and circumscribe the great principles on which the temple of liberty was being built. And if you have been taught doctrines conflicting with the great landmarks of the Declaration of Independence, if you have been inclined to believe that all men are not created equal in those inalienable rights enumerated, let me entreat you to come back, to return to the fountain whose waters spring close by the blood of the Revolution. Think nothing of me; take no thought for the political fate of any man whomsoever, but come back to the truths that are in our chart of liberty. You may do anything with me you choose, if you will but heed these sacred principles. You may not only defeat me for the Senate, but you may take me and put me to death, but do

not destroy that immortal emblem of humanity,—
the Declaration of American Independence."

And with what patient steadiness and self-posses-
sion did he pursue his great mission!

Moses was the very model of steadfast fortitude
and perseverance. Defiantly resisted, repeatedly un-
successful, and again and again foiled and mocked,
he continued the conflict, by argument, by expostu-
lation, by miracle, and maintained his ground with a
firmness of endurance which outwearied even Pharaoh's hardness. And when his own people lost
heart and confidence, and found fault with him, and
basely conspired against him, and God himself, by
reason of their unbelief, added to his charge and
difficulties, by deferring the fulfilment of the promise, he never once thought of giving up, but kept
to his work, reasoned, waited, and devoutly perse-
vered, till, from Nebo's top, he beheld the expected
land lying invitingly at his feet.

How like Moses, in these respects, was our late
President? Who ever encountered more or greater
perplexities, difficulties, provocations, and discouragements than those which beset his way? And yet,
with what earnest but passionless calmness did he
grapple with them! Look at him; unexpectedly
called from an humble sphere in which he had been
content to remain, and suddenly made the head of a
party for the first time, and, as it were, by accident,

coming into power, and as yet wholly without settled habits or traditions of official life, charged with the administration and maintenance of a government which one powerful state after another had renounced and repudiated, required to locate among a people who were almost all opposed to him, the subject of misrepresentation and unqualified abuse, waylaid for his life at almost every turn, mocked at for official awkwardness, maligned and resisted for his opinions and steadfast policy, tried by years of apparent failure before that policy obtained a single success, embarrassed by the zeal and boastfulness of his friends and subordinates no less than by his inexperience, and that of the country, in such a state of affairs, pressed on every side by some who could see no force in his obligations as a constitutional ruler, and cried down on the other by men whose sympathies with treason would allow of no measures large enough for the revolutionary emergency which had arisen, often forsaken by his friends, and deceived and censured and conspired against by those whom he had honored with his confidence; he patiently endured all, and stood calmly to the helm amid the shoals and tempests, never once giving way to anger, to resentment, to despondency under discouragements, or to intemperate exultation over the most rapid and brilliant successes, when at last they came. In all his extraordinary trials, and notwithstanding

his great solemn earnestness, his good nature, his
generosity, his kind feeling, and his wonderful meek-
ness, never once departed from him. Uncouth and
inexperienced as he was at the beginning, he knew
his place, and understood his own mind, and added
with every year to his force of character, his self-
possession, his executive capacity, and his magnani-
mous devotion, until there shone forth from under
that ungainly figure a grasp of principle, a directness
of judgment, a dignity of manner, a solemnity of
purpose, a goodness of heart, and a comprehensive
simplicity and justness of policy, which arrested the
attention and commanded the admiration of foreign
courts, and which place his name on the roll of earth's
best men and greatest rulers.

Some said that he was a tyrant. And if inflexi-
ble patriotic devotion, and the bold maintenance of
the majesty of law over self-will, unruly sectionalism,
and daring revolution, if untiring study and cou-
rageous promptness in bringing every power and re-
source of the Government into exercise for the over-
throw of armed conspirators and the preservation of
his country from ignoble dismemberment, if unquail-
ing confrontation of a subtle and mighty attempt to
destroy the most beneficent rule on the face of the
earth, if daring to use power to save a great and
useful nation at a moment when the last flames of
its life seemed to flicker for extinction, if these, and

such like instances of patriotic and Christian effort, constitute tyranny, then Abraham Lincoln was a tyrant.

But we have not so learned to count usurpation and tyranny. There is another spirit and style of action, of which there has much been seen and felt in recent years, to which these terms much more appropriately apply. It is the spirit which says of the black man, " If he complains of his wrongs, *lash him*," and of the white man, " If he stands in your way, KILL HIM." It is the spirit which comes to the Senate chamber with loaded canes, and answers patriotic logic with physical blows upon its author's head, to leave him dying in his seat. It is the spirit which enters defenceless towns in the guise of peaceful travellers, in order to rob, burn, and murder, out of mere brutish vengeance. It is the spirit which gathers infected clothing from the pest-houses, and sends them as honest merchandise to be distributed in unsuspecting communities, for the purpose of breeding death and desolation. It is the spirit which, with oaths in heaven registered to serve and defend, plots plunder, dismemberment, and revolution; which schemes in secret, and sends forth its emissaries in darkness, to burn unoffending cities unwarned, and to erase them, if it can, from the earth; which undertakes, in the name of freedom and religion, to subvert the very foundations of both, and to rear in their places an illegitimate thing, conceived in self-will, established by rebellion, and subsisted upon the forced toil of millions consigned to brutal degradation and eternal servitude. It is the spirit which incarcerates unfortunate prisoners of honorable warfare in pestilential holds, stifles them with thirst, starvation, diseased meats, if not slow poisons, and plants tons of gunpowder under them that, in case of inability to retain them, they might be blown to atoms at the mere touch of a match. It is the spirit which gets into the house of a sick public servant with a lie, and stabs him in his bed, and deals out slaughter to his unarmed and terrified attendants; and which, nothing daunted, holds the charged pistol to the head of the nation's legitimate chieftain, and blows out his brains in the presence of his family and friends, because it cannot overawe his noble purpose, nor drive him from his fixed fidelity to his country, his conscience, and his God.

Men and brethren, I may be mistaken; but if I have at all learned to estimate the character of human actions; if I have any true insight into the nature of human rights; if I have any just perception of what enters into the composition of the praiseworthy or the base, there is in things like these, the very quintessence of tyranny, and all its worst and most intolerable infamies. And I pity the man who cannot justify, or at least *excuse*, any stretching of

official power, however questionable in other circumstances, that may be requisite to save a free people,
and a government based on equal rights, from falling into the hands of such wrongful domination.
Rise from the little muddy circles of party politics
and prejudices, and look at it in the broad sunlight
of eternal morality, and see whether such " chivalry,"
fairly interpreted by its own acts, does not unmis-
takably belong to the sphere of the ugly, the brutal,
and the devilish.

It is not for me to say where the responsibility lies;
nor would I direct criminating words where they do
not apply. But these things are the true fruits of
secession, which show what it practically is, and in-
dex what I take as a full vindication of almost any
measures calculated to weaken and to vanquish the
unholy thing. If some were, by rigid construction,
extra-constitutional, they were not the offspring of
resentment and vengeance, nor of self-will, and vain
ambition, and love of power, which are the charac-
teristics of tyranny. If some were unprecedented in
the nation's history, so was the occasion which demanded them, and the treason which made them
necessary. And if, peradventure, certain provisions
of the Constitution, repugnant to its framers, and
applying only to sections which had, by deeds of re-
sistance and assault, forfeited their claims to its protection, were ignored, what good man would put his

country's existence in jeopardy, and imperil the cause
of freedom in all the earth, by endeavoring to uphold
what could but weaken himself, and strengthen those
who were at the time trampling the whole instrument under their feet, and glorying before the world
in their purpose to destroy it?

Silence as the antidote for traitorous proceedings,
and the Constitution to fetter the hands of conscientious loyalty in grappling with them, is a political
creed which argues ill for the patriotism of its confessors; but it embodies the exact logic of those who
look upon Abraham Lincoln as a tyrant. Another
man, an officer of the government, and sworn to defend it, may use his place to manipulate for that
government's destruction; he may go and levy war,
and raise armies, and make generals, and commission
agents, public and secret, to strike the death-blow to
its heart; and the Constitution, which ranks such
proceedings with earth's foulest crimes, is never
named. But when a God-fearing executive plants
himself in the way of the destroyer, and exerts his
proper power to save the most precious of political
creations, and gives promise of success in restoring
his country's unity, with its freedom enlarged, its im-
purities purged, and its greatness augmented, he is
denounced as a tyrant, and murdered for his devotion. Shame to such shallowness, and woe to the
guilt of such hypocrisy!

And whilst upon this point, let me quote a sentence or two even from that organ of our country's enemies, the London Times. " Abraham Lincoln," says that paper, in a recent issue, "was as little of a tyrant as any man who ever lived. He could have been a tyrant had he pleased, but he never uttered so much as an ill-natured speech. The war was attended with all war's horrors, but there was no cruelty at Washington. If the people of the seceding States were rebels, never was rebellion, except on the field of battle, more gently handled. In all America there was not one man who less deserved to be the victim of this revolution than he who has just fallen. He did nothing to aggravate the quarrel; short of conceding the independence of the South, he did everything to prevent or abbreviate it. He recognized it as his one great duty to preserve the Union, and whatever opinions may be entertained about the war and its policy, nobody can say that such a principle was otherwise than becoming in the President of the Republic." (April 29th.)

It would seem, however, to be one of the common laws in human affairs, that the most virtuous and useful men are the most hated and abused in their lifetime. This was remarkably illustrated in the history of Moses. How was he sneered at when first he appeared at Pharaoh's court! How did all Egypt despise him for his miracles! How did his own peo-

ple complain of him in their timidity, when they saw
the Egyptians coming upon them at Baal-Zephon!
How did they murmur against him at the waters of
Marah, and accuse him in the wilderness of Sin, and
cry out in condemnation of him at Rephidim! How
vexatiously did they depart from him while engaged
with God on their behalf, and rail at him, and take
up stones to destroy him in the plains of Paran!
How was he wronged by the conspiracy of Korah
and Dathan, and tried by the treacheries of Balak
and his apostate prophet, and mistreated at every
step of his self-denying career! And so it was with
all the prophets. Some of them were stoned, sawn
asunder, tempted, slain with the sword, " being des-
titute, afflicted." Even the blessed Saviour of the
world was crucified; his apostles were martyred; and
his great confessors, in every age, have been hunted
down with wrath and bloodthirstiness. Even among
the heathen, we find such men as Aristides banished,
Socrates poisoned, Demosthenes exiled, Cicero ex-
pelled and assassinated. And now, in this boasted
home of civilization, in these days claimed as the
culminating period of triumph for human rights, we
have to add to the list, the kind, generous, passionless, self-sacrificing, honest-hearted Abraham Lincoln, who in the midst of his wonderful achievements
for his imperilled country, and his great magnanimity
towards its foes and his, was sought out, and mur-

dered, for no other reason than that he was good and true and great.

He was but a man. God forbid that he should for one moment have a higher place in our affections or esteem than that which may lawfully be assigned to a man. I believe that there is real danger in these days, and one which is pointed out as the peculiar snare of the last times, of falling into a spirit of hero-worship, and an apotheotizing of human leaders, which is among the subtlest, easiest, and deadliest of idolatries. It was the great crime of some of the most enlightened nations of antiquity, and it will be the essence of the great apostacy under the Anti-christ. We need, therefore, to be carefully on our guard in that direction. But, let us not fail to do justice to the virtues of the dead, or refuse to keep in kind remembrance those whom God has honored as great servants of their kind.

It was a sublime work which Moses did for his people and for the world. He relaid the foundations of Israel's great nationality by new illustrations of God's covenant concerning them. He was the great reasserter of human rights over against the tyrannies of Egypt, and the great representative of Law at a time when the world had become oblivious to its high and immutable obligations. He was the great me-diator between Jacob's seed and their oppressors, and the friend who kept Israel from compromising their proper destiny. He was the great instrument in the Divine hand through whom deliverance was administered to an enslaved race. He was the great collector of the simple traditions of his people, and the reproducer of them for the enlightenment of mankind. And, taken all in all, he was one of those sublime mountains of human greatness from which new eras date, and the most important affairs of time take complexion and shape.

We are not yet in a position so well to understand the relations and importance of Lincoln's life and deeds. It remains for future ages to trace the bearings of his work upon the fortunes of humanity. But we know enough to warrant the remark, that generations to come will recur with grateful interest and holy reverence to the story of that rugged pioneer, coming suddenly from the wilderness to steer the greatest of the nations through the greatest of its perils, and to set an example of wise and prudent administration, worthy of the study and imitation of all the reigning powers on earth. Though never once setting up to be great, and seemingly unconscious that he was anything more than a man of the common average, history will not fail to write him down a great man and a model servant of his kind. Though occupying now no very exalted place in some men's estimation, his administration will mark a new era in the history of this continent, and

the time will come when his name shall be cherished by freedom's children as warmly as that of
Washington himself.

Had he left no other legacy by which to be favor-
ably remembered than the magnificent illustration
he has given of the value of talents which oft lie
hidden in the humbler walks of life, and of the ge-
nial excellence of institutions which throw open the
paths of honor and official greatness as well to the
low born and the poor as to the educated and the
rich, the world would still have reason to bless God
that he has lived. In this one respect alone there
gathers round his history an importance to which no
one can afford to be indifferent. The facts in his
career open a fountain of ever fresh inspiration to
improvement, fidelity, courage, and triumph, which
must give strength to many a fainting heart, and
fan the fires of generous ambition in many a lowly
spirit, and thrill and cheer to greatness and to good
many a one of whom the world otherwise would
never have heard, and teach the proud, the high-born,
and the wealthy, that their children are by nature
no better and no greater than the children of those
who serve in their houses, hew their wood, and draw
their water. There is, after all, an equality among
men, too prone to be forgotten ; and this fresh, in-
structive, and finished life, now added to the treasures of mankind, reopens and recalls the fact, and

sets it up on high for the everlasting encouragement of the lowly, and the thoughtful contemplation of all men.

This, however, is but a fragment of the case. Think of the terrific perils through which we have just passed; of the thunder-clouds of destruction which, time and again, threatened to overwhelm our homes and country in one common ruin; of the great feebleness to which the cause of loyalty, freedom, and humanity, had been reduced; and of the almost miraculous deliverance which has been vouchsafed. Think of the gigantic proportions, far-reaching influences, and subtle sophistries of that long-organizing movement, which must be henceforward known as treason and rebellion; of the universal ignorance of the resources and real mightiness of those despised States to which the preservation of the Union and the maintenance of the General Government's sovereignty were left; of the quietus which has been given to the exultations of the hirelings and friends of despotic and aristocratic power at the prospect of America's humiliation; and of the shame which has been made to overtake the insulting babblings of foreigners touching the follies of the North. Think how, in the midst of discouragements and disasters on sea and land, the contest for the majesty of law, national unity, and equal rights was maintained, until rebellion was defeated in its

disorganizing aims, disrobed of its pride and usur-
pations, and bereft of its ill-directed power. Con-
sider where this great nation of ours this day stands
in the estimation of the world, and how sublimely
it is rising up to the true greatness of its earliest
manifestos, with one of its greatest stains and most
troublesome causes of difference and dissension as
good as purged away forever, and the great motto
of "LIBERTY AND UNION, ONE AND INSEPARABLE,"
nailed to its flag-staff, and woven with its emblem-
atic colors, to signal hope to the oppressed of every
land; and, when you have searched out the agency
by which such great things have been wrought, and
found the earthly well-spring of those successes
which half the world believed to be impossible, all
will be seen connecting with a name till recently as
humble as it will henceforth be great, and radiating
from the meek heart, the calm judgment, the wise
administration, and the patriotic fidelity of ABRAHAM
LINCOLN.

And this is the man against whom it has been in
the hearts of some to plot schemes of assassination,
and, with a malignant effrontery for which the Eng-
lish language has no name, to carry into execution.
Alas! for which shall we lament the most,—the loss
which has been inflicted by the audacious murder,
or the awful depravity and bloodthirstiness which it
shows to be lurking in the hearts of men who would

fain have us believe them to be our country's truest friends? Both are subjects for our profound grief; but for both we have this great consolation left, that a just God is upon the throne of the universe, and that He will bring every work into judgment, with every secret thing, whether it be good or whether it be bad.

I will not undertake to maintain that our late Chief Magistrate made no mistakes, or that he never erred in his estimates of men or adoption of measures; even Moses himself did ill-advised things, and was censured of God for his conduct at the waters of Meribah.

Neither do I conceive of all the surroundings in which the assassin found him, as good, pious, or becoming a Christian's dying-place. He was but a man, lacking in experience in public affairs, and of that meek and generous nature which was, perhaps, too willing, in smaller matters, to acquiesce in the tastes and wishes of people less conscientious than himself.

But, in the great elements of his character, he was just, devout, Christian, and of a moral make and stamen, to which few in politics have ever attained. He believed in God, in Revelation, in Christ, in prayer, in the necessity of virtue, in providence, and in the habit of settled dependence upon the precepts and administrations of Heaven; and his creed was per-

haps quite as real, as influential, as practical, as that
of any who venture to sit in judgment upon him,
and certainly as much so as that of thousands who
give tithe of mint, anise, and cummin, but are not
quite so particular in the weightier matters of judgment, mercy, and faith. God is his judge, and in
His hands I am hopefully willing to leave him. If
he was not so eminent a saint, he was an honest
friend of his country, a sincere sympathizer with the
suffering and the lowly, and a great servant and
benefactor of mankind. If he was shot down in a
theatre, he died a martyr to his country and to principles which good men in every age will honor and
approve.

It is time, my friends, that I should dismiss you;
but indulge me with yet a remark or two, before I
conclude. The public mind is a good deal exercised
about monuments and memorials to our deceased
chieftain. Now, the greatest honor that can be rendered to his memory is for those who revere him to
stand by the principles for which he lived and fought
and died,—to reproduce his good, honest purposes
and generous nature in themselves,—to steer by those
landmarks which guided him to greatness. Other
monuments will perish. The memorials constructed
of nature's elements will pass away with nature's
wastes. At best, they are but mute things, the
meaning of which may be lost even while they yet

stand. But great principles and truths, practically wrought into immortal minds, and lived into the histories of mankind, will endure through all the ages, and keep telling their impressive story forever.

Moses is dead, and to this day no man has ever seen his sepulchre ; but his genius lives, fresh, vigorous and active, and will continue to live on, increasing in dominion as the race expands and men are found to accept his ideas. No monumental piles could so perpetuate his honor.

Nor can the fame of Lincoln wane, or his potent greatness fail in its power on the earth, if men will keep to the channels of thought and action again laid open in his life.

And if there was that in him worthy of honorable commemoration, the nearest to immortality that we can give it is, to live it and act it ourselves, and to teach our children to do the same. If his ideas and convictions were framed to the statements and precepts of Revelation, and yielded fruits worthy of our honor, that honor is best rendered by giving to that self-same Revelation full sway in all our thoughts and reasonings. If he considered it bad policy, and a crime which cannot escape Divine indignation, to withhold from a fellow-being his native rights, and we think him entitled to our praise for his consistent and conscientious adherence to that belief, we shall praise him most effectually by making it the basis of

our actions too. If he regarded all men as of one
blood, and entitled by their Maker to the same rights,
and acted out to sublime distinction the golden rule,
to do to others as we would have them do to us, and
the credit of his course calls for significant celebra-
tion, we cannot answer the call in better form than
to take the same into our souls as the inviolable law
of our lives. If his great devotion to his country's
unity, and his patient self-sacrifice for its preservation, demand some marked acknowledgment from
his countrymen, there is no way in which that acknowledgment can be more handsomely made, than
by the earnest and honest copying of his example.
If he held secession to be treason, and felt it as a
solemn obligation upon his conscience to make no
compromises with it or with the doctrines of its de-
fenders, and men would honor his judgment and
scruples in the case, let them cling to these teachings as their political creed, and see that they are
enthroned among the inviolable stabilities of our
cherished institutions. And if he had no double
conscience, one for private life, and another for political conduct, but for all his relations kept to the
one great and ever-binding law of right and conscience, and you think it meet to give honorable ex-
pression to your appreciation of such simple integ-
rity, the sublimest thing to be done is, conscientious-
ly and always to conform your course to the same

Divine standard, and live to truth and right and God, in business and in politics, the same as in your charities and in your church.

But whether any are moved or not by such reference to the dead, let us not forget, that we all have obligations upon us, and duties to discharge, and responsibilities to meet, in the directions indicated, which take their rise from our very position in the universe, and which it is our great business in this world to learn, acknowledge, and obey.

We may be humble, feeble, and unnoticed in the great crowd of men; but we are each God's workmanship. He has put each of us here for a purpose; and we each must some day answer to Him for the manner in which we have fashioned our lives, and fulfilled our mission.

We may not have nations to lead, or to organize to new ideas, or to guide and keep in the hours of trial; but we each have spheres of importance in which to operate, and little gardens which we ourselves alone can cultivate, and webs of little deeds to weave, in which our highest life is to be found.

We may not, indeed, be Moseses or Lincolns, but, like both of them, we can be ourselves; and by being honestly our true selves in humble things, we know not to what high spheres we yet may be raised. We have the highest authority for it, that faithfulness in that which is least, is faithfulness also in much. We know by whom, and to whom, it was said, "Well done, good and faithful servant; thou hast been faithful over a few things, I will make thee ruler over many things." (Matt. 25 : 23; Luke 16 : 10.) And both the histories of the men whose names I have associated in these remarks, preach and illustrate the same hopefulness.

> " Lives of great men all remind us
>   We can make our lives sublime,
> And, departing, leave behind us
>   Footprints on the sands of time—
>
> Footprints that perhaps another,
>   Sailing o'er life's solemn main
> A forlorn and shipwrecked brother,
>   Seeing, shall take heart again.
>
> Let us then be up and doing,
>   With a heart for any fate;
> Still achieving, still pursuing,
>   Learn to labor and to wait."

III. THE CLOSING SERVICES.

THE FINAL PRAYER.

ALMIGHTY GOD, the eternal Source of wisdom and purity, from whom all good counsels, all holy desires, and all just works do proceed; sanctify our hearts by Thy holy Word. What we know not, teach Thou us. Whatever is wrong in us, help us to overcome, and to put far from us. Whatever in us is good, aid us in cherishing, and in carrying forward to perfection. Enable us to go forth into the world with the spirit of true religion in our hearts, and to spend all our days in Thy fear and love. May Thy Gospel ever be precious to our souls. And when Thou shalt see fit to remove us from this state of toil, trial, and danger, may Thy grace avail for us, and the gates of eternal life open to receive us, through Jesus Christ, our Lord, and our Hope. AMEN.

THE CONCLUDING HYMN.

"Guide me, O thou great Jehovah !
Pilgrim through this barren land ;
I am weak, but thou art mighty,
Hold me with Thy powerful hand," &c.

www.ingramcontent.com/pod-product-compliance
Lightning Source LLC
Chambersburg PA
CBHW021435090426
42739CB00009B/1493